Seymour Simon

SEE MORE READERS

DANGER! VOLCANOES

SeaStar Books · New York

This book is dedicated to Michael and Debra.

Special thanks to reading consultant Dr. Linda B. Gambrell, Director, School of Education, Clemson University. Dr. Gambrell has served as President of the National Reading Conference and Board Member of the International Reading Association.

Permission to use the following photographs is gratefully acknowledged:
front cover: © Bernhard Edmaier/Science Photo Library, Photo Researchers, Inc.; title page: © Krafft/HOA–QUI, Photo Researchers, Inc.; pages 2–3: © David Weintraub, Photo Researchers, Inc.; pages 4–5: G. E. Ulrich, Hawaiian Volcano Observatory, U. S. Geological Survey; pages 6–7, 10–11: J. D. Griggs, Hawaiian Volcano Observatory, U. S. Geological Survey; pages 8–9: © Stephen and Donna O'Meara, Photo Researchers, Inc.; pages 12–13: © Pat and Tom Leeson, Photo Researchers, Inc.; pages 14–15: Donald A. Swanson, USGS; pages 18–19: © Galen Rowell/CORBIS; pages 20–21: © Michael T. Sedam/CORBIS; pages 22–23: © Wolfgang Kaehler/CORBIS; pages 24–25: © Georg Gerster, Photo Researchers, Inc.; pages 26–27: © Bill Ross/CORBIS; pages 28–29: © Sólarfilma; pages 30–31: © Carol Cohen/CORBIS; page 32: © James A. Sugar/CORBIS.

Library of Congress Cataloging-in-Publication Data is available.
ISBN 1-58717-181-3 (reinforced trade edition)
1 3 5 7 9 RTE 10 8 6 4 2
ISBN 1-58717-182-1 (paperback edition)
1 3 5 7 9 PB 10 8 6 4 2
PRINTED IN SINGAPORE BY TIEN WAH PRESS
For more information about our books, and the authors and artists who create them,
visit our web site: www.northsouth.com

The biggest explosion in nature
is a volcano's eruption.

An erupting volcano shoots out
a hot melted rock called lava.
A volcano is a hole in the ground
that lava comes through.
A volcano is also a mountain
formed by the lava when it cools.
About fifty volcanoes erupt
each year around the world.

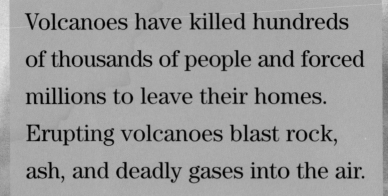

Volcanoes have killed hundreds
of thousands of people and forced
millions to leave their homes.
Erupting volcanoes blast rock,
ash, and deadly gases into the air.

They also can cause dangerous
slides of lava, rock, ash, mud,
and water.
A large eruption can destroy
an entire city and even change
the weather.

We get the word "volcano" from
Vulcan, the Roman god of fire.
Today, we know that a layer
of rock called the crust
covers our planet.
Deep beneath the crust
the temperature rises to
more than a thousand degrees.
That is hot enough to melt rock.
The melted rock, called magma,
flows through cracks in the crust.

When magma reaches the surface
of the earth, it is called lava.
As lava cools it hardens
to form rock again.
Rivers of fiery lava can destroy
buildings, cars, and almost
anything that is in their path.
But lava usually flows slowly
enough for people to get out of
the way.

Sometimes magma can get
trapped inside a volcano.
For more than 100 years
Mount St. Helens was a quiet,
peaceful volcano.
But in March 1980, clouds of
ash and steam began to blow
out of the top of the mountain.
Then, on the morning of
May 18, the volcano exploded.

In seconds, one whole side
of the mountain was blown away.
Ash, steam, and rock flew outward
at speeds of 600 miles per hour.
Many thousands of trees were
knocked down like toothpicks.
Hundreds of houses and miles of
roads were destroyed.
Nearly 60 people lost their lives.

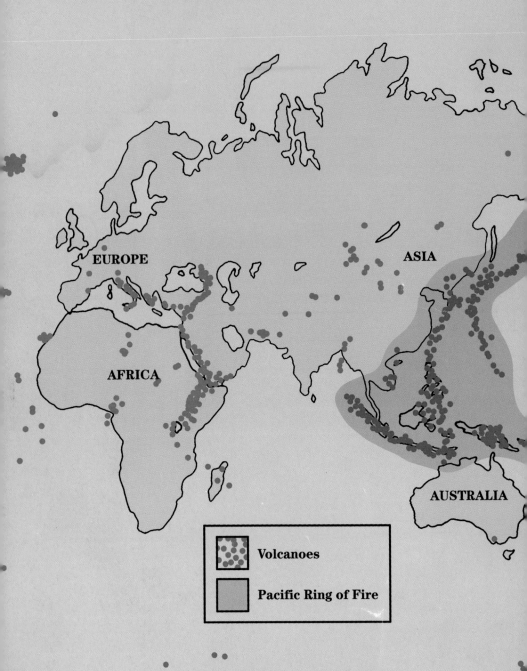

EUROPE

ASIA

AFRICA

AUSTRALIA

Volcanoes

Pacific Ring of Fire

There are more than 500 active
volcanoes around the world.

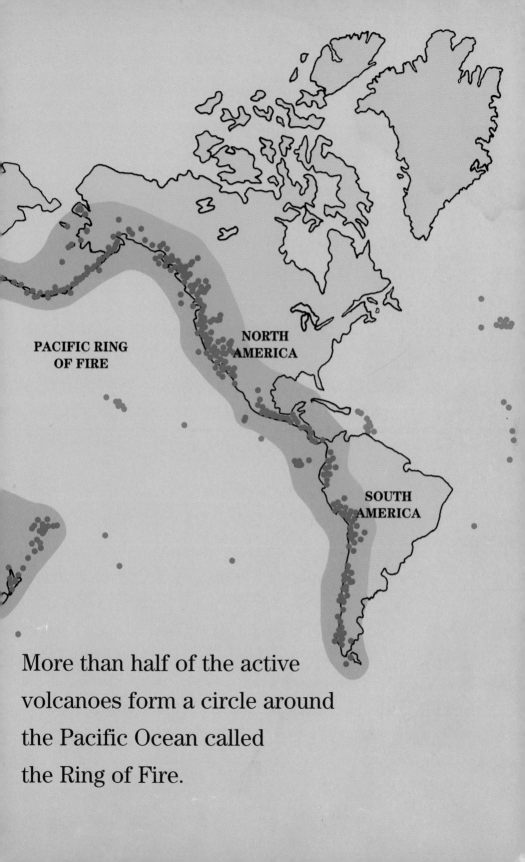

**PACIFIC RING
OF FIRE**

**NORTH
AMERICA**

**SOUTH
AMERICA**

More than half of the active
volcanoes form a circle around
the Pacific Ocean called
the Ring of Fire.

In 1943, magma started shooting out through a hole in a field near the Mexican village of Paricutín. Ash and bits of burnt rock called cinders fell to the ground around the hole.

In a few months, a steep mountain
of cinders grew to over 1,200 feet.
Cinder cone volcanoes
are the most common kind
in North America.
This is the Santa Ana Volcano
in El Salvador.

Many layers of hardened lava
form some volcanoes.
A broad, gently sloping cone forms
in a shape like a warrior's shield.

Mauna Loa in Hawaii is
the world's largest **shield** volcano.
It is 70 miles wide and the top
is more than 30,000 feet
above the ocean floor.

Dome volcanoes grow
when a trapped pool of lava
swells inside a mountain.
Lassen Peak in California
and Mount Pelée in Martinique
are lava dome volcanoes.
Mount Pelée exploded in 1902,
killing 30,000 people
in a nearby town.

Most of the volcanoes in the world are formed by layers of rock, lava, cinders, and ash. Mount Fuji in Japan and Mount Shasta in California are **composite** volcanoes.

Around the world are many very
old volcanoes that no longer erupt.
They are called extinct volcanoes.
Crater Lake in Oregon
is an extinct volcano,
with water filling its top.

Some volcanoes are quiet
for hundreds of years
before they erupt again.
They are called dormant volcanoes.

Volcanoes erupt and destroy.
But volcanoes also build up the
land and build islands in the sea.
Most of Earth's surface comes from
millions of once-active volcanoes.
There is a good chance that the
ground beneath your feet comes
from a volcano that was active
in the past.

When a volcano erupts, lava
or cinders cover the ground.
It looks as if all plants and animals
are gone forever.
But in a few short months,
living things return.
Plants grow in the cracks, and
insects, birds, and other animals
come back.

Volcanoes do not just destroy.
They create new land
on planet Earth.